WHAT'S INSIDE

POJO'S UNOFFICIAL
ULTIMATE GUIDE TO
POKÉMON

Charmander CP ???

- **The World's Hottest Game**
- **How-tos, Tips, and Strategies**
- **PokéStops, Gyms, Lures, and More!**
- **Pocket-sized for Quick, Easy Reference on the Go!**

HOW TO CATCH 'EM ALL!

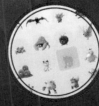

This book is available in quantity at special discounts for your group or organization. For further information, contact:

Triumph Books LLC
814 North Franklin Street
Chicago, Illinois 60610
Phone: (312) 337-0747
www.triumphbooks.com

Printed in U.S.A.
ISBN: 978-1-62937-404-8

Editor in Chief: Bill Gill, a.k.a "Pojo"
Graphics Designer: Phil Deppen
Writers: Scott Gerhardt, Adam Motin, and Bill Gill
Cover design: Preston Pisellini

INTRODUCTION

What Is Pokémon GO?

Pokémon GO is an "augmented reality" game, blending the real world and the Pokémon world into a playable adventure on your mobile device. Players visit real world locations in order to discover Pokémon, catch Pokémon, battle other Pokémon trainers, and look for Pokémon-related items.

Pokémon GO is a free-to-play mobile app for iPhone and Android devices. It is what many people call a "freemium" game. It's completely "free" to download and play. But you also have the "premium" option to buy in-game currency called Pokécoins. Pokécoins can be used to purchase additional Pokéballs and other items. Pokécoins are not needed in order to play Pokémon GO, however. The game is thoroughly enjoyable without spending a dime.

Pokémon GO works using your device's GPS, and marks your current real world location. The GPS puts your avatar onto a cartoony version of Google Maps. Your avatar is a cartoony version of you. The maps are extremely detailed, showing roads, buildings, houses, rivers, parks, signs, monuments, etc.

The next requirement in the game is that you actually get outside and move! The maps will show Pokémon rustling about in bushes, and PokéStops you should visit, and Gyms you should go to. It's all pretty amazing if you ask us. And it's your job to "catch 'em all" and "visit 'em all"!

So...What Is Pokémon?

We've been Pokémon experts at Pojo since 1998. We started a Pokémon site 18 years ago, and it's still up and running today. But we realize that this might be the first time some of you are playing a Pokémon-themed game. So here is a little Pokémon history lesson.

Satoshi Tajiri of Japan is credited with creating Pocket Monsters / Pokémon. He loved catching insects and tadpoles as a kid in the suburbs of Tokyo. When he first saw the Nintendo Game Boy system and Link Cable, he imagined insects traveling across the link cable to other Game Boys. He pitched his idea to his friends at Nintendo. Nintendo funded his project. Satoshi Tajari then spent six years developing the game that would ultimately become Pocket Monsters Green and Pocket Monsters Red in Japan. Red and Green were released in 1996, and Pocket Monsters was a huge success in Japan. Due to trademark issues, the name was shortened to "Pokémon" for the North American release.

Pokémon Red and Blue were

released simultaneously in North America in 1998. They are the granddaddies of all Pokémon games. The games appear to be simple children's games, but are actually very deep role-playing games (RPGs). The games feature a ton of strategy and a dynamic storyline.

In the Pokémon RPGs, you are a trainer trying to catch the variety of pocket monsters (Pokémon) that appear in the game. Once caught, Pokémon can be added to your party and trained to assist you. The longer you train Pokémon, the more attacks they learn, and the stronger they become. Various versions of Pokémon Red and Blue have been released over the years, amassing over 57 million units of sales. In total, the Pokémon franchise has sold over 279 million copies of Pokémon-themed games!

An old Pokémon game that is somewhat similar to Pokémon GO is a game called Pokémon Snap. Pokémon Snap was released on the Nintendo 64 way back in 1999. In Pokémon Snap, you played a Pokémon photographer named Todd Snap. The premise of this game was that you rolled through various Pokémon environments in a cart on a track, and took photographs of Pokémon for Professor Oak. We know it sounds lame, but it was a ton of fun and extremely addictive. After each Rail Ride, Professor Oak gave you grades on your photos. You kept trying to photograph all the Pokémon you could and tried to get better shots on each pass. You had some items at your disposal to interact with the Pokémon environment while riding along, like a flute, apples, and Pester Balls. People loved Pokémon Snap. You could even take your game cartridge down to the local Blockbuster video store and print your pictures out as stickers.

Pokéfans over the years dreamed of a real world version of Pokémon Snap, and started making YouTube videos merging the Pokémon world into the real world. Some of these videos are extremely creative if you want to Google them.

Next in line was a little-known game called **Pokémon Dream Radar**. This game was released in 2012, and was the first Pokémon game to use Augmented Reality (AR). You used the camera on your 3DS as a view finder and walked around your house. He also used the 3DS system as a radar. Dream Clouds would sometimes appear, partially blocking your view on the screen. You would clear the Dream Clouds off your screen like a first-person shooter. Occasionally the cleared Dream Clouds would reveal Pokémon to capture inside your house. This game was a fun little diversion and only cost about $3.

In the fall of 2012, Niantic and Google created an app called "Ingress" for Android phones. Ingress is an AR, multiplayer, online-location-based game. The game has a story line

based in science fiction. Ingress is like a giant game of Capture the Flag. You pick one of two sides: the Enlightened or the Resistance. The game plays in real time and in the real world. You attack enemy portals, protect your own portals, collect Exotic Matter, and a whole lot more. One cool aspect about Ingress is that players can suggest Portal locations— statues, buildings, paintings, tourist spots, etc. Niantic would evaluate the suggestions, and add them into the game. The game has been installed on over 10 million Android devices.

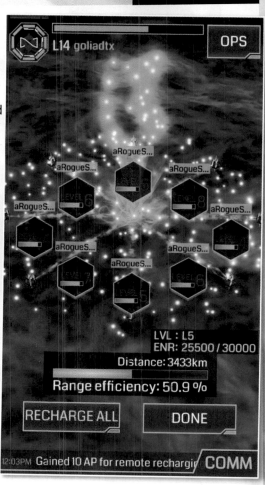

Enter Pokémon GO!

In 2015, Nintendo and The Pokémon Company Group announced that they would work with Niantic to create Pokémon GO, a global location-based game where you could go out into the real world and catch Pokémon. It was a plan to marry Niantic's Ingress gaming engine with the awesomeness of the Pokémon franchise. *Pojo Note: Many of the Portals, and Exotic Matter spawn sites, in Ingress serve as PokéStops and Pokémon spawning points. Some clever Pokémon collectors fired up Ingress on their phones to find places to catch rare Pokémon in Pokémon GO!*

Pokémon GO was released in the United States on July 6th, 2016. Within 10 days it was biggest mobile game in U.S. history, passing Candy Crush's 2013 popularity in active users. As we write this guide, Pokémon GO currently has about 21 million active users each day! The game is currently more popular than Netflix, Twitter, and Pandora.

What makes Pokémon GO so appealing?

One reason is that Pokémon GO does a pretty good job of replicating the core components of the Pokémon franchise in the real world. You see Pokémon in the wild and you catch Pokémon in the wild. Just like Jules said in *Pulp Fiction*, you need to "walk the earth" in order to catch 'em all. "You know, like Caine in *Kung Fu*. Just walk from town to town, meet people, get in adventures." If you follow Jules' advice with the Pokémon GO app, you'll have a great time!

Another appeal of Pokémon GO is the social impact. You can play this game while you are out and about with friends and family. You can go for a walk in the park and catch Pokémon together and share the experience. You can attack Gyms as a team and feel a sense of joint accomplishment.

Another appeal is the power of nostalgia. Many of the people playing Pokémon GO are in their 20s and 30s and 40s. In

1998, they were in elementary school, or high school, or college when they were playing the original Pokémon games. They know all of the original 151 Pokémon in the game by heart, and they want to "catch 'em all" again!

And yet another appeal is that it's completely FREE! You don't have to spend a penny to enjoy Pokémon GO!

Enter Pojo's Pokémon GO Pocket Guide!

We know that Pokémon GO is now reaching a huge audience, and that some of our readers have no idea what Pokémon is or what a Pokédex is. Some of you do not have a clue what to do at Pokémon Gyms. And you might not have any idea what a Pokémon Combat Chart is, and what Pokémon are best to attack with. Many old-school Pokémon players know this stuff right off the top of their heads from years of Pokémon gaming experience, but many simply do not.

So we've created this guide to walk you through everything you need to become a Pokémon GO master! You don't get an instruction manual with Pokémon GO, but you have one now! We'll walk you through catching your first Pokémon, to evolving your first Pokémon, to taking down a Gym Leader. We explain everything in the game.

If you haven't tried Pokémon GO yet, there is no need to be intimidated. Download the app, read our guide, and get out there and exercise, and "catch 'em all!"

SAFETY FIRST!

First and foremost—always be aware of your surroundings! You probably have already heard many stories about people being injured while playing Pokémon GO because they weren't paying attention, from people falling, to people walking into traffic, to kids falling off skateboards. It's one of the first screens you see while loading the Pokémon GO app, so heed the warning!

There are a lot of things safety can mean though, besides not falling off a bridge:

- If you're going on a long hunt in the sun, wear sunscreen!

- Make sure you have drinks and snacks with you in case you start feeling hungry or thirsty. You can sometimes be out for hours, so you need something in case you start to feel weak.

- If you're crossing the street, make sure you pay attention to the cars—do not assume they will automatically see you and stop. You might have the right of way, but if they aren't paying attention you might be in danger.

- Be careful about going to dark places alone, like alleys. You may be hunting Pokémon, but someone there might be hunting your wallet, so make sure your surroundings are safe.

- Always wear bright colors at night. If other people can't see you, they can't avoid you.

- Have backup battery power. The last thing you want is to walk a very, very long way expecting to use a map to get back, and your phone dies.

- And last but not least—NEVER play while driving a car or riding a bike. No Pokémon is worth it!

HOW TO GET PIKACHU AS YOUR STARTING POKÉMON!

At the very beginning of the game, you get the option of starting with one of three different Pokémon: Charmander, Squirtle, or Bulbasaur. This is exactly how you would have started playing Pokémon Red or Blue way back in 1998. But what if you want to be like Ash Ketchum in the anime? Did he start with one of those three? No! He had a Pikachu, and if you use this little tip, you can too!

When you first start playing Pokémon GO, you are presented with the three Pokémon options mentioned above. But instead of picking one at this point, just walk away. That's right—pick a direction, any direction, and start walking in a straight line until you get past them.

Eventually, they will respawn in front of you. Just keep on walking. When they spawn the third time, you guessed it—keep walking. But this is Pokémon GO, after all—get used to a lot of walking!

Once the starting Pokémon spawn the fourth time, if you look around, they will now give you a fourth option: Pikachu! Who wants to start with Fire, Water, or Grass when you can start with Electric! Of course, if you would rather start with one of the other three that's okay too—over time you should have a chance to capture all of them, so it's not like you can't get the other ones later. But if you want to be just like Ash, don't wait until later—get your Pikachu first!

MAIN SCREEN

The Main Screen is where you will spend most of your time, so make sure you are well acquainted with it. The person, known as your Avatar, walking in the middle is you! The game map always tries to keep you centered and moving in the same direction you are actually moving in the real world. However, the GPS can be a little off sometimes when you first start the game. Once you start walking a straight line outside, the GPS should be very close to your actual location.

The map you see is the augmented world around you. If it looks like water in the game, you're probably near water. If it looks like you're near a path in the map, you probably are near a path. Now, one thing we have found is that not every path is a road. Sometimes it might be a hiking trail, or a bike path, or something else you can't drive on.

The compass is in the upper right corner. The red arrow always points north, so it's easy to always know which way you are going. You can always tap on the north arrow to change your perspective. You can also slide your finger across the map to change your perspective as well. And you can pinch in or out to zoom in or out.

In the bottom right corner is your Nearby Screen, showing you the three closest Pokémon to you. Touching it brings up the full Nearby Screen, which we will discuss elsewhere in this book. The bottom left is your name, avatar, level, and how close you are to the next level. Tapping this will take you to the Name Frame screen. Last is the Pokéball in the bottom center, which takes you to your main menu.

NAME FRAME SCREEN

The Name Frame Screen is a great place to keep up with how you are progressing in the game.

You first see your name at the top and your full avatar below, which you can swipe left and right to rotate so you can see your sweet backpack. Under that is your level, plus how much XP (experience) you have, and how much XP you need to reach the next level.

The button below that is your Journal, which shows the last 50 things you have done and what time they happened. This is either collecting from a PokéStop, catching a Pokémon, or letting a Pokémon get away.

Below that you see how many Pokécoins you have, the day you started, and which team you are on.

Phone screen

●●○○ AT&T 🛜   2:50 PM   🡱 100% 🔋

TheGamersDome

Level 22

31241 / 100000 XP

JOURNAL

210

START DATE:
7/7/2016

Team Instinct

Underneath all of that are your Awards. You'll get them for how far you've walked, how many Pokémon you get in the Pokédex, how many total you have caught, and how many you have evolved. You can see how many Eggs you've hatched, how many PokéStops you've visited, plus how many Gym battles you have won and how many times you have trained at your own Gym. The next 14 Awards are all for catching certain kinds of Pokémon, and the last two are specifically for catching CP 10 Ratatas for Youngster and how many total Pikachus you have.

Everything you could ever want to know (or brag to your friends) about your exciting journey can be found here on this screen!

NEARBY SCREEN

For the Pokémon collector who loves the thrill of the hunt, the Nearby Screen is your best friend. Clicking on the banner in the bottom right of the Main Screen will bring up the full Nearby Screen. This is where you can see the nine closest Pokémon to you. If you've never seen a particular Pokémon before, you will only see a shadow image of it. Each one has a number of footsteps, and this marks how far away you are from the Pokémon.

- No footsteps means a Pokémon is 0m to 40m away. This is what is called the "Action Radius"—the radius from which you can trigger Gyms and PokéStops. If a Pokémon has zero footprints, it will likely appear on the screen any second.

- One footstep means the Pokémon is 40m to 75m away.

- Two footsteps means the Pokémon is 75m to 150m away.

- Three footsteps means the Pokémon is 150m to 225m away.

Once you have this information, you can start to track your next Pokémon!

Pokémon proximity first goes from left to right—left is closest. Then the proximity goes from top to bottom—top is closest. If you see a Pokémon getting closer to the top left, then you're getting closer to that particular Pokémon. If a Pokémon moves to the bottom right, you are getting farther from that particular Pokémon. Chasing Pokémon down this way is like being on a football field and playing the classic children's game "Hot and Cold." If a Pokémon's footprints go from 3 to 2, "you're getting warmer!"

Always track in a straight line for the best results. With some practice, you can track down any Pokémon you want!

POKÉDEX SCREEN

The Pokédex is where you can learn all about the Pokémon you have caught. Each Pokémon corresponds to an individual number. This goes back to the old Pokémon Red and Blue video game days. There were 151 Pokémon in Red and Blue, matching the number in Pokémon GO. *We have all the Pokémon numbers in the Pokédex in the back of the book to help you!*

You can also see the numbers of Pokémon you haven't seen yet. If you encounter a Pokémon at least once, there will be a shadow in the Pokédex where it belongs. The Pokédex won't tell you much except the number and name, and how many times you've seen it.

If you have caught that Pokémon, you get to see a lot more information. The Pokédex will show you how many you have seen and caught, as well an average weight and height for the Pokémon. It will also show you what type of Pokémon it is, such as Fire, or Psychic, or Ground. It will also teach you a little more about that Pokémon.

In addition, if the Pokémon has an Evolution, you can see it there. If you have not seen the Evolutions, though, it won't tell you anything about them. For example, if you have seen Charmander, but not Charmelion or Charizard, then you will see question marks and shadows for those two.

If you want to see exactly how many Pidgeys or Ratatas you have seen, this is where you can find out! Plus, that knowledge will tell you how close you are to "catching 'em all."

POKÉMON SCREEN

The Pokémon Screen is one of the most useful screens in the game! There you can sort your Pokémon in many different ways.

The first thing to note is that when you click on any Pokémon you have, you can touch the star in the upper right corner and it will mark it as one of your favorites, which is great for being able to sort them later.

You have six options when sorting Pokémon:

- First is by most recent, so you can tell what you have caught lately. Also, if you opened an Egg and didn't realize it, the recent screen can help you figure that out!

- Next is by favorite, so all those Pokémon you marked previously can now all be sorted together so you can see them all at the same time.

- Sorting by number will show you the Pokémon in the order they are in the Pokédex.

- If you want to know who your biggest Pokémon are, you can sort by HP—Hit Points

- If you just want to sort them alphabetically, you can do that by name, which makes it easier to "clean up" your Pokémon Bags and trade Pokémon you no longer need for Candy.

- Finally, if you want to you can sort by CP, which will show the overall combined "Combat Power" of that Pokémon. That way you'll know who will be the strongest competitor in a Gym.

81° ✉   📍 ✳ 🔇 📶 📶 85% 🔋 10:29 a.m.

RECENT

FAVORITE ☆

NUMBER #

HP

NAME A-Z

COMBAT POWER CP

EGG SCREEN

The Egg Screen displays information about all the Pokémon you have in Egg form that you haven't been able to hatch yet. You can hold up to nine eggs at a time.

For each Egg, you will have three different distances marked: 2km, 5km, and 10km. Each distance refers to how far you have to walk each of those Eggs to hatch them. To hatch an Egg, however, you first have to put it into an Incubator, which you will find on your Items page. An Incubator can only hold one Egg at a time. To incubate and hatch multiple Eggs at the same time, you can purchase additional Incubators in the Shop.

Once you have walked the entire distance required to hatch an Egg, the Hatching Screen will show up and hatch the Egg. The longer the distance, the better chance you have of getting a rare and powerful Pokémon, but nothing is guaranteed. You can sometimes get good stuff from a 2km Egg and sometimes bad stuff from a 10km—you never know until they hatch.

Once an Egg hatches, you will eventually get a replacement from a PokéStop. Unfortunately, you can't get rid of Eggs you don't want—you have to hatch them. So, if you have a bunch of 2km and 5km Eggs and you want a 10km Egg, your only choice is to hatch the low ones and hope to get a 10K Egg from the next stop. Eggs also come with a lot of Candy, so it's a great way to power up a Pokémon fast!

Tip: Make sure you have the Pokémon GO app open while you walk. Kilometers walked when the Pokémon GO app is closed won't count toward hatching your Eggs.

POKÉMON | EGGS
112 / 300 | 8 / 9

0.8 / 2.0 km   4.3 / 5.0 km   1.8 / 5.0 km

1.8 / 5.0 km   0.0 / 5.0 km   0.0 / 5.0 km

0.0 / 5.0 km   0.0 / 2.0 km

SHOP

The Shop will let you buy supplies you need using Pokécoins. You can earn Pokécoins by defending Gyms, or by spending real money. (We discuss defending Gyms later in our guide.) So what can you buy with Pokécoins?

- The first thing you can buy is Pokéballs, but we don't recommend buying Pokéballs unless you are really desperate. You can load up on Pokéballs just by going to PokéStops. If you absolutely need them, they come in lots of 20 (100 coins, 5 coins each), 100 (460 coins, 4.6 coins each), or 200 (800 coins, 4 coins each).

- You can buy one Incense (80 coins), or a group of eight (500 coins, 62.5 coins each) or 25 (1,250 coins, 50 coins each) at a discount.

- You can purchase Lucky Eggs, which are priced the exact same as the Incense.

- Lure Modules come in a single (100 coins) or an 8-pack (680 coins, 85 coins each). You can only get Egg Incubators as singles for 150 coins. We have found these to be the thing we spend our coins on the most because they help you progress quickly.

- The Shop will also allow you to purchase upgrades for your Items' Space or your Pokémon Storage for 200 coins each. You should be able to manage Items without having to buy extra space, but we have found that you will probably have to upgrade Pokémon Storage as you get deeper into the game, especially on longer hunts.

- You can purchase coins with your real money in increments of 100, 550, 1,200, 2,500, 5,200, and 14,500. The values get better the more you buy in bulk, with the highest being about a 30% discount over the smallest.

SHOP

 0

 0

ITEMS

20 POKÉ BALLS   **100 POKÉ BALLS**   **200 POKÉ BALLS**

 100   460   800

INCENSE   **8 INCENSE**   **25 INCENSE**

 80   500    1250

POKÉSTOPS

Whenever you visit a PokéStop or can even touch to click on it, it will bring up the PokéStop screen. You can get some good information from this screen.

The top of the screen shows you the name of the PokéStop. Touching it will open a larger image of the stop, and many have additional information about the stop itself listed there. Since a lot of stops are historical markers or various works of art, this is neat way to learn more about the area you are hunting in. You might actually get a better appreciation for things you pass all the time and take for granted.

Below that is a very small white oval. This is where you would put a Lure Module, or where you will see a Lure Module if it has been added. By touching it, you can install a module if you are close enough, or it will show you the name of the person who installed the module if one is already there. This gives you a chance to thank him or her if you know who it is.

The smaller picture of the PokéStop is below (in the disc) so you can identify it. Interacting with this disc is the way you get supplies. Simply swiping across the screen spins the disc, giving you supplies. You do not have to touch the supplies to get them—they are added automatically.

Finally, if the stop is too far to interact with, a pink oval will appear under that picture saying "This PokéStop is too far away," letting you know you need to get closer in order to use it.

Liberty Bell Slot Machine
Charles August Fey began inventing... >

LIBERTY BELL SLOT MACHINE

Joseph L. Kauffman Memorial Monument
Erected in March of 1919 by Walter P. Temp... >

Walter Temple Bust

Walter Temple Bust
3:52 PM

GYMS SCREEN

The Gyms Screen provides all the important information about what is happening at a Gym. To enter a Gym and start competing, you must reach Level 5 and then join a team: Valor (red), Mystic (blue), or Instinct (yellow). Try to join a team that your local friends are in.

Each Gym has a level which corresponds with its Prestige. The level tells you how many slots there are for defenders; those slots increase as Prestige increases. A Level 3 Gym, for example, will have three defenders, and all those Pokémon are from different Trainers.

Next, the screen shows the Pokémon that are actually in the Gym. The biggest CP Pokémon will have a crown over their name. They will be the last Pokémon in the Gym as it loses Prestige. If you don't see a crown, you can swipe left and right to see all of the Pokémon in that Gym. It displays the name of the Pokémon and its CP.

To the right is the name and avatar of the person holding the gym, with their level listed behind their name.

At the bottom right is the Battle button, which allows you to select which of your Pokémon to send into battle. If your team controls a Gym, you might see a button on the bottom left with an arrow and a plus sign. This means that your team can put another Pokémon in that Gym, so you can add yours by hitting that and selecting one.

CATCHING POKÉMON

When you have found a Pokémon and are ready to catch it, a new screen pops up.

You will see the Pokémon with its name and CP right above it. In the bottom center of the screen, you will see the Pokéball you are going to toss at it, as well as how many Pokéballs you have. This screen gives you a bunch of other options as well.

At the top left, there is an icon of a man running. This button lets you run away from the Pokémon and you will stop trying to catch it. In the upper right, there is a toggle button for turning the Augmented Reality option either on or off.

At the bottom right you will see two icons. One is the camera, which allows you to take a picture of your Pokémon. The picture will only show the Pokémon itself, not its name or CP, along with your Trainer name. The icon below that will allow you to switch Pokéball types or feed the Pokémon a Razz Berry.

Once you place your finger on the Pokéball, you will be able to flick the Pokéball at the Pokémon in order to catch it. This gets easier with practice. Once you've become more experienced, you can get an additional bonus by spinning the Pokéball and tossing a curveball, but this can be tough. You also get an XP boost and a higher chance to catch the Pokémon when the circle around him is at its smallest point.

Each Pokémon has different colored "toughness rings" surrounding them, too: Green = Easy; Yellow = Moderate; Red = A Mighty Foe! Tougher Pokémon might knock down or blow your Pokéballs away at times. You'll want to use stronger Pokéballs on stronger foes.

AUGMENTED REALITY

We briefly discussed Augmented Reality (AR) earlier in this book. There are a lot of differences between trying to catch Pokémon with AR on and with AR off.

With AR on, you will see the Pokémon in the real world around you. Moving yourself and the camera left, right, up, and down will change where the Pokémon is, possibly even moving them off screen. The Pokémon will be at a fixed GPS point in the real world. If the Pokémon is off screen, arrows will appear on the side telling you which way to turn to see the Pokémon again. You have to hold your phone pretty stable to be able to catch Pokémon with the Augmented Reality turned on.

With AR off, the Pokémon will always be in the middle of the screen no matter how you stand or what direction you face. This is helpful if you are near someone's house, so that you won't have to turn the camera toward the house to catch a Pokémon. Otherwise, the home owners might wonder why you're hanging around in their front yard!

Catching with AR on is more fun but also more challenging, so practice with it turned off until you get the hang of it.

Turning AR on also creates an opportunity for great pictures. You can take a photograph with a Pokémon standing next to a friend or with a pet. You can also find wacky places to take a picture of Pokémon. Taking Pokémon pictures with the AR on takes some practice, but can also be a ton of fun.

With time, you'll also get good at toggling that AR switch based on your environment.

We took two screenshots of Gastly for you, 15 seconds apart. One with the AR on, and one with it off. Both were taken inside.

Joltmammer

Joltmammer

Spearow CP 141

26

46% 4:44 PM

Zeldaliana

ITEMS SCREEN

On the Items Screen, you can see exactly which Items you own and how many of each you've acquired (with the exception of Egg Incubators, for some reason). Each Item has an explanation of what it is and the inventory count. You also will have a trash can next to each Item, allowing you to get rid of Items you don't want or need to have.

At the very top of the screen, you'll see how many slots you have used and how many you have left available. If you start to run tight on space, you should trash some stuff to make room for more important items, especially Pokéballs. We have found that the items we most want to trash are Revives, Razz Berries, and lower-level Potions. Never trash all of them, though!

If you are near a Gym, you could battle a bunch to get rid of Potions and Revives without wasting them. But our experience has been that we always have way more Razz Berries than we need.

Never get rid of Incense, Lucky Eggs, Pokéballs, or Lure Modules. These Items are way too useful and cost Pokécoins to buy. And don't forget, your camera also counts as an Item— but you can't get rid of it or any Egg Incubators, not that you would want to anyway.

ITEMS

130/350

Potion

A spray-type medicine for treating wounds. It restores the HP of one Pokémon by 20 points.

x48

Revive

A medicine that can revive fainted Pokémon. It also restores half of a fainted Pokémon's maximum HP.

x30

Incense

Incense with a mysterious fragrance that lures wild Pokémon to your location for 30 minutes.

x4

Poké Ball

A device for catching wild Pokémon. It's thrown like a ball at a Pokémon, comfortably encaps... its target.

x38

Lure Module

POKÉBALLS

Pokéballs are the single most important item that you can have in Pokémon GO, and also the item you will run low on the quickest.

When you first start out, you will get plain old Pokéballs, which are just fine. Early on most Pokémon will not break out of their balls, so normal Pokéballs are up to the task. As you start to level up and encounter Pokémon with more CP, they might break out of their balls. No big deal—you can usually just throw another one and try again.

Two factors will determine how much trouble it will be to keep a Pokémon in its ball. The first is the color of the circle in the middle of the Pokémon. Green means it should be pretty easy. Yellow is going to be a little harder. Red means there is a good chance it will break out. The other factor is the size of the circle. The smaller the circle, the more likely they will stay in the ball, but also the more precise a throw you need to capture them.

As you level up, you will get Great Balls at Level 10 and then Ultra Balls at Level 20. These more powerful Pokéballs just make it easier for a Pokémon to remain captured. Master Balls have a 100% capture rate and are best used against the hardest-to-find Pokémon. We know the Master Balls themselves are very rare. Also, as of this writing, we do not know what level you need to reach to acquire Master Balls, as no one has publicly caught higher than Level 30.

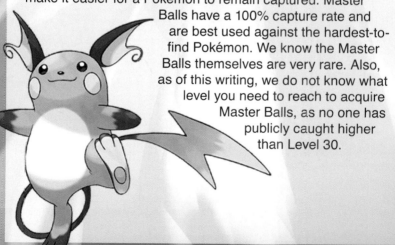

Charmander / CP ???

LUCKY EGGS

Lucky Eggs are a great way to level up faster because they double the XP (experience) you gain for 30 minutes. You should get a Lucky Egg when you achieve Level 9.

When you are first starting out, we recommend using a few Lucky Eggs to gain a lot of XP quickly. This can rapidly get you to better Pokémon and get you a lot of supplies. As you continue to level up, however, you will find that the amount of XP you gain from a Lucky Egg in relation to the amount you need to level starts to get really bad, especially once some Pokémon start breaking out of their balls multiple times.

There is a still a really good trick to using Lucky Eggs to get thousands and thousands of extra XP. It's something we call the Evolution Trick.

When you collect and transfer Pokémon, you will get a lot of Pokémon Candy. You are going to want to stockpile as much as you can until you can evolve about 60 Pokémon at one time. The best Pokémon for this are Pidgey, Weedle, and Caterpie, who only need 12 candy to evolve.

Once you've built up, use a Lucky Egg and then evolve your Pokémon as fast as you can. We have found that you can evolve about 60 Pokémon in 30 minutes. Since you get 500 XP per Pokémon you evolve (1,000 XP if it's new), evolving 60 will give you an extra 30,000 XP! That is getting the best value from your Lucky Eggs.

You will get free Lucky Eggs when you reach Levels 9, 10, 15, and 20. Other than that, you'll have to buy them with Pokécoins.

Lucky Egg

A Lucky Egg that's filled with happiness! Earns double XP for 30 minutes.

EXCHANGE FOR   80

POTIONS AND REVIVES

Once you get to Level 5 and battling in Gyms, you will need those Potions and Revives you have been stockpiling.

As you battle, you are going to have Pokémon get injured and even knocked out. You will need a way to get those Pokémon battling again. Whenever Pokémon are knocked out, you will need to use a Revive to get those Pokémon back on their feet. When used, it will not only revive them but will give them back some of their HP.

To heal an injured Pokémon and get more HP, you need to use Potions. Initially you will get Potions that will heal the Pokémon for 20 HP. Once you hit Level 10, you get Super Potions, which will heal your Pokémon for 50 HP. Finally, at Level 15 you will get Hyper Potions, which will heal a Pokémon for a whopping 200 HP.

Most Pokémon will be healed with one Hyper Potion; if they have a lot more than average HP, such as Chansey or Snorlax, it might take two or three. By the time you get to Hyper Potions, you will find that regular Potions don't do enough and you will likely just trash them to keep your bag clear for other items. If you know you are going to do a lot of Gym battles, make sure you are well stocked on Potions first, and you might have to heal as many as six Pokémon after a battle.

ITEMS
193/400

Potion

A spray-type medicine for treating wounds. It restores the HP of one Pokémon by 20 points.

x5

Super Potion

A spray-type medicine for treating wounds. It restores the HP of one Pokémon by 50 points.

x18

Hyper Potion

A spray-type medicine for treating wounds. It restores the HP of one Pokémon by 200 points.

x63

Revive

A medicine that can revive fainted Pokémon. It also restores half of a fainted Pokémon's maximum HP.

x38

Poké Ball

LICENSE AND LURE MODULES

You can always go out walking to find Pokémon, but sometimes it would be nice to have the Pokémon come to you.

That is where Incense and Lure Modules come in handy. Both of these items will cause the Pokémon to be more attracted to you, but both do so in different ways, and it's important to understand the differences. Both items will last for 30 minutes.

The Incense will cause Pokémon to be attracted toward you, no matter where you are. You are surrounded by a pink circle which shows the Incense is working. At least once every five minutes, you should see a Pokémon in the area that has the same pink circle around it. This Pokémon cannot be seen by other GO players in the area, just you. If you are moving at a quick pace, the Pokémon come more quickly—up to one per minute, so once you start Incense, keep moving!

Lure Modules, though, reward you for not moving. Lure Modules must be installed in a PokéStop. Once initiated, pink petals will rain over the PokéStop. Like Incense, Lure Modules bring Pokémon to you, but unlike Incense, the Pokémon that show up appear for all GO players in the area, making this great for a group of people. Make sure you stay near the PokéStop, though—if you walk away, you won't see the extra Pokémon anymore.

Both Incense and Lure Modules are fantastic for farming Pokémon when you want a bunch of Candy or Stardust, too!

Incense

Incense with a mysterious fragrance that lures wild Pokémon to your location for 30 minutes.

EXCHANGE FOR 🪙 80

Lure Module

Modules that attracts Pokémon to a PokéStop for 30 min. The effect benefits other people nearby.

EXCHANGE FOR 🪙 100

RAZZ BERRIES

As you level up, you are going to find Pokémon with higher and higher CP, which means they will be harder and harder to catch. Eventually you will find Pokémon that are very hard to catch even with Great Balls and Ultra Balls. When that happens, you are going to need a little something extra—after all, you don't want that legendary Pokémon to appear and then have it run away.

When you need that something extra, reach into your bag and pull out a Razz Berry. A Razz Berry will make Pokémon about one level easier to catch. It will usually turn yellow circles into green circles, and red circles into yellow circles. You don't even have to be stingy with them—you will usually find more Razz Berries than you need from PokéStops. They are also prime for being deleted when you need to free up space, so don't be afraid to use them.

Once used, Razz Berries will work for one successful throw. If you catch the Pokémon but they escape, you will need to use another Razz Berry to affect the next throw. If you miss, though, the Razz Berry is still working. The game will not let you use a Razz Berry unless it is useful to you, so don't worry about using one when you don't need to.

You will receive some Razz Berries as a reward for Reaching Level 8. Razz Berries will also start appearing at PokéStops when you reach Level 8 as well.

THE POKÉMON CAMERA

The Camera is one of the cooler items that you have in your bag, and the resulting photos you get are different from just capturing screenshots. If you've been on social media, you've surely seen some great Pokémon GO pictures. People have put Pokémon into real life situations and done it flawlessly and fluidly.

To do this, make sure that the AR (Augmented Reality) toggle button is turned on, or you're not going to see any of the world around you. The switch is in the upper right corner of your phone when you are in the "Capture Pokémon" screen.

When you go to capture the Pokémon, make sure you are pointed in the exact direction of the Pokémon, because you won't be able to move the Pokémon around. In the bottom right, hit the Camera button, which will bring up a traditional

camera screen with the shutter button at the bottom. Once you have everything lined up the way you want it, you can take the picture.

If you like the image, hit the checkmark to save it. If you don't like it, hit the trash can. If you do checkmark it, then it will save the image to your phone's picture gallery, just like any other photo.

The Camera will clean up the picture by removing on-screen game buttons. It also puts your Trainer name at the bottom right of the picture, which is really cool because then anyone you show it to will know that you took it.

The only times you'd want to do a screenshot instead of using the Camera is if you want the Pokémon's name and their CP displayed in the picture, or if you want to show your friends a screenshot of a great area you've found with lots of PokéStops.

SETTINGS SCREEN

The Settings Screen is where you can change some of the main settings for the game.

If you'd rather play with the music off, you can. Some people like listening to their own music while playing, which the game lets you do.

Next you can turn off sound effects, and the button after that is vibration. We don't recommend turning either of these off. Both are great clues for when you're near a PokéStop, leave a PokéStop, or find a Pokémon.

Pokémon GO can be a battery hog on long walks. A nice feature in the Settings is the Battery Saver mode. This will get you more gameplay out of your battery. Switch on Battery Saver and the phone will go almost completely dark when you turn it upside down. This will also remove the graphics while it is down, since you can't see them anyway. This is a fantastic setting to save battery life and doesn't affect the quality of your experience. You also might want to go into your phone's menu and disable the Auto-Lock setting that turns your screen off after a certain amount of time to make sure you're not missing any Pokémon.

You can also check to opt out of any emails, as well as a few quick links to give you the quick start tips again, show you the help center, report an issue, or sign out of the game.

SETTINGS

Music

Sound Effects

Vibration

Battery Saver

Send Pokémon GO–related events, promotions, offers, and news updates to my email address.

Quick Start

Help Center

Report High-Priority Issue

About Pokémon GO   0.29.2

Sign Out

ITEM MANAGEMENT

When you start a Pokémon GO game, you will have 350 spaces in your bag available. After excluding the Camera and the infinite-use Egg Incubator, that leaves 348. If you manage your Items correctly, you should never need to purchase additional bag space.

Here is a great set of guidelines on how to best manage your items:

- First, keep an eye on your inventory count. Once you get in the 300 range, you should begin to take action. Since you can get up to eight items from a PokéStop, you can reach the 350 maximum pretty quickly. If you reach 350 Items, then going to a PokéStop will give you nothing, and since you want as many Pokéballs as possible, that's not a good thing. You should look over your items at this point and get rid of some of the nonessentials.

- Unless you are planning on spending some time at a Gym, you likely have way more Revives than you need. You should probably get this down to 15 or 20 total.

- Potions are next. We would take it down to 25 or 30 of your single best Potion, or use your top two if you don't have 25 or 30 of the top end.

- Lastly, Razz Berries tend to be very plentiful and are seldom used as often as you get them. A good guideline is to keep the number of Razz Berries equal to your level, up to Level 19. Once you hit Level 20, keep about 1½ times your current level, because breakouts are very common there.

After following these simple rules, you should have plenty of room for Pokéballs!

56

ITEMS
235/400

Potion
×2
A spray-type medicine for treating wounds. It restores the HP of one Pokémon by 20 points.

Super Potion
×3
A spray-type medicine for treating wounds. It restores the HP of one Pokémon by 50 points.

Hyper Potion
×76
A spray-type medicine for treating wounds. It restores the HP of one Pokémon by 200 points.

ITEMS
235/400

Razz Berry
×35
Feed this to a Pokémon, and it be easier to catch on your next throw.

Camera
When you encounter Pokémon the wild, you can use to photograph them

Egg Incubat
A device that incuba you walk until it is re Unlimited use!

Egg Incubat
A device that incuba you walk til it is re Breaks uses.

ITEMS
235/400

Poké Ball
×42
A device for catching wild Pokémon. It's thrown like a ball at a Pokémon, comfortably encapsulating its target.

Great Ball
×9
A good, high-performance Poké Ball that provides a higher catch rate than a standard Poké Ball.

Ultra Ball
×14
An ultra-high performance Poké Ball that provides a higher catch rate than a Great Ball.

Lure Module
×2
A module that attracts Pokémon to a PokéStop for 30 min. The effect benefits other people nearby.

Razz Berry

TRANSFERRING POKÉMON TO PROFESSOR WILLOW

As you go on Pokémon expeditions, you are going to catch a lot of Pokémon.

A lot of those Pokémon will be duplicates of ones you have already captured, and some will have really low CP. Those are not going to do you a lot of good in terms of leveling up, so your best option is to transfer them to Professor Willow to free up space for more valuable Pokémon.

In return for the transfer, the Professor will give you back one Candy of that Pokémon type. While it's not a lot, it certainly adds up over time and is very important for both evolving and leveling up your Pokémon.

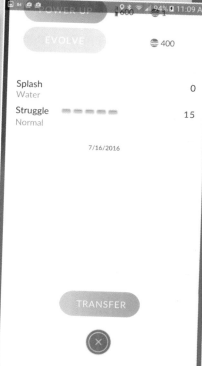

Some people will see the same Pokémon over and over and think, "I don't need to catch this—I have already caught a lot these." Not true at all! Those Pokémon you capture are going to give you a ton of Candy over time, which will let you evolve a whole bunch and get a ton of XP.

For example, to evolve a Magikarp into Gyarados, you need 400 Candies! You're going to need to catch 101 boring Magikarp in total if you want a Gyarados. (Catching a Magikarp gives three candies and transferring to Professor Willow another one.)

We're not even sad to see a Pidgey, because we know each one is almost like getting about 125 bonus XP once we evolve them! So make sure you collect a bunch of the Candy—it's one of the biggest keys to becoming a high-level Pokémon Trainer!

Note: The transfer button is at the bottom of each individual Pokémon's screen.

LEVELING UP AND POWERING UP

Leveling up and powering up your Pokémon is a fantastic way to get higher CP Pokémon. But it requires both Stardust and Candy to do it.

As your Pokémon's Combat Power gets higher, the amount of Stardust and Candy necessary to power them up goes up as well. As tempting as it might be, we would strongly advise all Pokémon Trainers not to power up your Pokémon until at least Level 15—and that's only if you plan on mostly doing Gym battles. Otherwise, hold off until you've reached Level 20.

Until Level 20, you will gain levels pretty quickly, and gaining levels means catching Pokémon with a higher CP in the wild. Once you hit Level 20, however, it becomes a lot harder to level up further. So if you use all your Candy and Stardust on a Pokémon early, you could very easily find a Pokémon in the wild shortly after with even better CP—with no Stardust or Candy available. If you are a patient Trainer, you can have an absolutely huge Pokémon army just from catching wild Pokémon.

You are limited on how high you can train a Pokémon based on your level. There is a dot on the semi-circle behind your Pokémon. The closer it gets to the bottom right, the closer you are to its maximum training for that level. Once you level up, you can go back and make it bigger. Just remember that patience is a virtue, and if you're going to spend Candy and Stardust, you want that Pokémon to be good for a long time.

CP348

HP 55 / 55

Normal	95.44 kg	1.42 m
Type	Weight	Height

11747
STARDUST

6
TAUROS CANDY

POWER UP   800   1

Zen Headbutt   15
Psychic

Earthquake   60

EVOLVING POKÉMON

Once you have enough Candy, you are going to want to evolve some Pokémon into their higher forms. Evolving works a bit different from leveling, though, so read on!

First, no Stardust is consumed by evolving, only a lot of that Pokémon's Candy.

Second, know that you will gain XP from evolving. Evolving a Pokémon gives you 500 XP, and if it's new to your Pokédex, you will get 1,000 XP. Evolving can certainly be a great way to get a lot of XP fast and start shooting up levels. Also, no matter what level you are, you are going to get the same XP, so you don't have to save these for later levels. However, as we mentioned in the Lucky Egg section, holding a bunch of Pokémon evolutions until you can do many at once combined

with a Lucky Egg is the single fastest way to level. So be patient and get the biggest bang for your evolution.

Stage 2 Tip—Because you get higher CP Pokémon as you evolve, you are always going to want to go from Basic to Stage 2 all at once. This means, for example, that if you want your Charizard, wait until you have 125 Candy and then evolve from Charmander to Charmeleon then straight to Charizard.

Why wait? As you level, you can capture bigger and bigger Pokémon in the wild. The bigger the Pokémon, the bigger its evolution. So, why start early with a 100 CP Charmander and evolve into a 400 CP Charmeleon? And then wait a long time until you get more candies and evolve into an 800 CP Charizard? *Better:* Start with a wild 800 CP Charmander, then immediately evolve into a 1,500 Charmeleon, and then evolve into a 2,500+ Charizard. The only way to get more Candy is to get more of that Pokémon, so you'll be able to pick your single best Charmander to start with.

ATTACKING GYMS

We generally that find new players have the most trouble mastering Gym battles, and the basic strategy behind it. The game doesn't go a great job of explaining it, but we are here to help!

First of all, Gyms on the GPS map can be one of four colors, each of which refers to the team that controls that Gym. Yellow, blue, and red represent Team Instinct, Team Mystic, and Team Valor, respectively. If it is white, that means nobody controls it, and the first team to put a Pokémon there will control it. To do that, tap on the Gym and there will be a button in the bottom left. Hit that button and then choose a Pokémon—it's that simple. How you interact with colored Gyms, however, depends on whether or not you control it.

If your Team does not control the Gym, then you can go into battle with a team of six Pokémon of your choosing. Once you have selected your Pokémon, you will then battle against the Team that controls that Gym. For every one of their Pokémon you knock out, their Gym will lose a little Prestige. If you knock all the Pokémon out, then their Gym will lose a lot of Prestige and will probably kick out their weakest Pokémon. The next time you battle, you will need to defeat one fewer Pokémon, making the battle easier. This gives you a lot of XP as well, so it's not so bad when a rival controls a Gym.

If your Team does control the Gym, then you can train your Pokémon there. In this case, you select only one Pokémon and then battle as long you can

09:00

Cupid's Span
Gym level 2

2000 / 4000

CHARMANDER

CP 36

sara

against the Pokémon there. For each one you defeat, your Gym will gain a little Prestige and you gain a little XP. While the XP is better fighting against a rival Gym, if you can get a Pokémon into a Gym and keep it there for 20 hours, you get to collect free Pokécoins and Stardust, so you definitely want to put a strong Pokémon in the Gym. The higher the Gym Prestige, the higher the level, and the more Pokémon that can be in the Gym.

Actually fighting involves learning how to use a few moves. To use the Pokémon's basic move, just tap on the screen. It really doesn't matter where you tap, though we prefer near the middle so we don't accidentally hit another button. If one of the blue bars next to your name is full, you can use your Pokémon's Special Attack by pressing the screen for one second. Keep in mind that doing so will use up the energy in that bar.

Your opponent's Pokémon is automatically attacking you as well, so you are going to want to avoid getting hit if you can, especially from Special Attacks. To do this, swipe quickly left or right. This will cause your Pokémon to move left or right to dodge an attack. Practice enough and you can avoid a lot of your opponent's attacks.

Gym fights occur in real time, and everyone who is fighting a certain Pokémon will all damage it at once. This is where you can

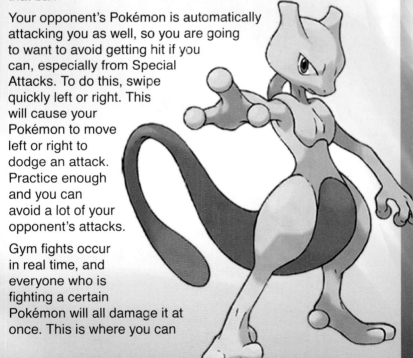

use teamwork to take down even the biggest of Gyms. Before fighting, everyone should prepare their teams, and then try to initiate the battle at about the same time. If you time it right, all of you can enter the fight at the same time, and you will tag-team attack the Pokémon there. While some high-level Gyms may be hard to attack alone, using two, three, or even more people to attack the defending Pokémon at once will make a huge difference in your total damage and how fast they get knocked out. It's also a great way for all of you to earn a ton of XP quickly!

Another thing that can make a huge difference is matchups. Your Pokémon can be weak or strong versus the Gym defenders based on their Type. So you want to try to maximize these matchups when setting up your attacking team. You can see what Pokémon are in the Gym, so prepare your team accordingly. Later in the book is a Combat Chart that shows you the best attacks to use against various Types of Pokémon.

Remember that each Pokémon, even those with the same name, can have a number of different attacks that could be of different Types. Keep this in mind when leveling and also when choosing your Pokémon for battle. Getting good matchups will allow you to take down Pokémon with a lot more CP than you. Take some time to study and soon you'll be controlling your own Gym!

SUPPORTING LOCAL BUSINESSES

As you are exploring and playing Pokémon GO, you will see that lot of PokéStops and Gyms are actually local businesses, either inside them or near them.

Now, if you are just passing by outside and want to collect from that PokéStop, that is completely fine. If you are going to sit down because there is a Lure Module or something else there, however, you need to be respectful of that business. This especially goes for restaurants. If a restaurant has enough people come in and not order anything, they will likely refuse to let Pokémon players inside anymore. You are using their facilities, so you need to do your part to support them. If you want to sit there, consider getting a meal or an appetizer, or at least a drink. That makes you a paying customer and will make the business happier to support Pokémon players.

We have even seen businesses who will give bonus discounts for Pokémon players, so you can take advantage of that while you are there. We're not saying you have to spend a lot of money every time you go, but you should support a business that is supporting you. If they weren't there, their business wouldn't have a PokéStop and you wouldn't have a place to collect supplies and put Lure Modules. This is a great way of saying thank you to them.

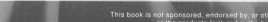

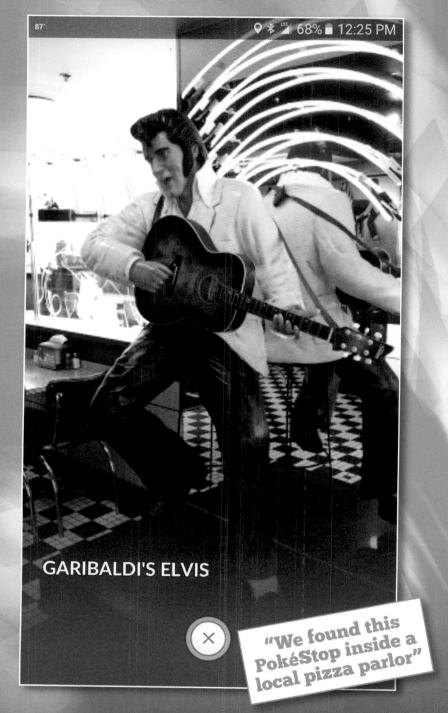

GARIBALDI'S ELVIS

"We found this PokéStop inside a local pizza parlor"

SOCIALIZING

One of the best aspects of Pokémon GO is the opportunity to be around a lot of other people while you're out playing the game. That is very different from most video games, where you usually are playing by yourself, even if you're online. While you can certainly try to do everything on your own, you will find that talking to, and making friends with, other people will help a lot in your Pokémon GO journey.

Sometimes you will come across some rare and hard-to-find Pokémon. When you do, you can ask other GO players if they have seen it and know where it is. We have found people to be very nice in this respect, and it has led us to catching Pokémon we might not have found. Plus, you never know when you might make a new friend out there, and Pokéhunting is always more fun when you do it with friends.

Sometimes your better half might not play Pokémon GO, but they enjoy walking, and they will keep you company. Sometimes you can hunt down Pokémon as a team, and spread out across parks and fields to help narrow the search. Sometimes you'll want a big group of friends to help you take down a Gym. And it's always easier to take funny pictures if you can include your friends in them.

On the flip side, do your best not to be rude to people. Don't have your phone's volume turned all the way up without headphones. Don't run into people to go catch a Pokémon. If you do, apologize quickly for it. Being kind and polite will get you a whole lot further than being rude.

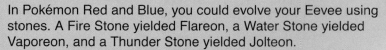

In Pokémon Red and Blue, you could evolve your Eevee using stones. A Fire Stone yielded Flareon, a Water Stone yielded Vaporeon, and a Thunder Stone yielded Jolteon.

During the first season of the Pokémon Anime (1998), Ash Ketchum encounters "The Battling Eevee Brothers." The brothers are named Sparky, Rainier, and Pyro.

- Sparky has an Electric Eevee Evolution—Jolteon
- Rainer has a Water Eevee Evolution—Vaporeon
- Pyro has a Fire Eevee Evolution—Flareon

They are pushing their younger brother Mikey to evolve his Eevee into something. But Mikey ultimately decides to keep his Eevee as a loveable little Eevee, and of course his little Eevee takes down Team Rocket and saves the day.

When you normally evolve an Eevee in Pokémon GO, you will randomly get a Jolteon, Vaporeon, or Flareon. There are no "Eeveelution Stones" in Pokémon GO. But quickly, people found out that if you name your Eevee after one of the Battling Eevee brothers from the anime, you can control your Eeveelution!

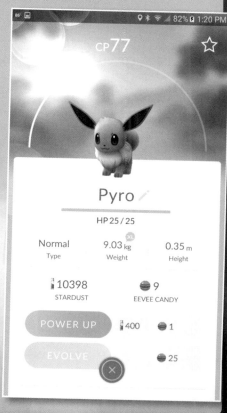

If you want a particular Eeveelution, you must rename your Eevee before you evolve it. (You should probably also log out of the game and back in just to make sure the name change was recognized by the Pokémon GO servers).

Then rename your Pokémon:

- Sparky for Jolteon
- Rainer for Vaporeon
- Pyro for Flareon

After you log back, you can evolve away!

Pojo Note: This Eevee trick is considered finding an "Easter Egg" in Pokémon GO. The CEO of Niantic teased that there are other Easter Eggs still to be found within the game! Try something wild, maybe you'll be credited with the discovery!

TAKING FUN PICTURES

We discussed taking pictures with your camera earlier, and this is one place where you can really get creative. When a Pokémon appears with your AR turned on, try to think of a funny or ironic way to take its picture.

We saw someone take a picture of the horse-shaped Ponyta on top of a dog. Maybe you find a Magikarp at sushi restaurant. Maybe a Koffing or a Weezing is near a garbage can. Writer Scott Gerhardt took one of Psyduck next to a real duck.

This is an area where your imagination can just run wild. Try to come up with the funniest pictures you can think of, and then share them with your friends or put them on social media so lots of people can enjoy them. There are Twitter accounts that are nothing but people who have taken funny Pokémon GO pictures. You can laugh at those, and maybe it will give you some inspiration.

Now, you certainly don't have to do this kind of thing, and if it's not something that appeals to you, then don't feel like you are obligated. But taking funny pictures is just another reason why Pokémon GO is taking the world by storm!

Unphf

POKÉMON GO IN THE NEWS

Since the game's release, Pokémon GO has not only become one of the most downloaded mobile games of all time, it's also been dominating the headlines. Each day features a news story focusing on the game's popularity, the adventures Pokémon Trainers have gotten into, or the creative ways people are using the game. Here are just a few:

Reports said that within two days of its release, Pokémon GO had been installed on more than 5% of all Android devices in the U.S. In its first week of release, it became the all-time most downloaded app on the App Store. By July 20, 2016, more than 30 million people had downloaded the game worldwide. The average daily usage of the app on Android devices in July 2016 surpassed those of Snapchat, Tinder, Twitter, Instagram, and Facebook.

A man in Brooklyn, New York, claimed to be the first person to catch all 142 Pokémon available in the U.S. He said it took him exactly two weeks to "catch 'em all."

The Durham Bulls, a minor league baseball team in North Carolina, has invited Pokémon GO players into their empty ballpark when the team is on the road. For $5, Trainers are welcome to walk around the field and catch as many Pokémon as they can. Proceeds are being donated to a local pet adoption charity.

During a press briefing at the U.S. State Department, spokesman John Kirby called out a reporter who was playing Pokémon GO when he should have been listening. Kirby said, "You're playing the Pokémon thing right there, aren't you," to which the reporter replied, "I'm just keeping an eye on it."

In one of the first large-scale Pokémon GO meetups, about 5,000 people gathered in Chicago's Millennium Park to hunt Pokémon on July 17. More than 100 similar meetups have been scheduled since then from coast to coast.

Some of the creative inventions seen in the news include Poké Glo, an illuminated button that makes players visible in the dark; the Poké-Han, a plastic necklace that holds your phone in front of your face; and PokéVision, an app that allows players to enter in an address and see all of the Pokémon around it.

REGIONAL POKÉMON

Pokémon GO encourages you to explore your area and catch as many Pokémon as possible, but you probably haven't had to travel very far outside your usual neighborhood.

Unfortunately, there is an exception to this rule. As of this writing, there are four Wild Pokémon that are specific to certain continents.

- Tauros is only in North America
- Farfetch'd is only in Asia
- Mr. Mime is only in Europe
- Kangaskhan is only in Australia

This is bad news for people who are really trying to catch all the Pokémon in the game. To be honest, we have no idea why they did regional exclusives. It seems like even after they implement trading, you will probably have to trade in person, so it could be very difficult to get one of these Pokémon.

But don't give up hope, good Pokémon Trainers out there! There is still another way for you to catch all of these Regional Pokémon without a bunch of plane tickets!

Remember those Egg Incubators? Well, luckily all four of these Regional Pokémon have a chance to hatch from a 5km or 10km Egg! It will probably take you quite a few Eggs to catch all three of them, but that's just a little more walking you have to do, and you get a Stay-in-Shape bonus!

WHAT'S INSIDE AN EGG?

We told you all about Pokémon Eggs and how to hatch them. And now you're probably wondering, "What's inside Pokémon Eggs?"

Well, you will get a Pokémon, some XP, some Candy, and some Stardust. Based on reports from around the globe, these are the Pokémon you can find in each type of Egg.

2km Pokémon Eggs:

Bulbasaur, Charmander, Squirtle, Caterpie, Weedle, Pidgey, Rattata, Spearow, Pikachu, Clefairy, Jigglypuff, Zubat, Geodude, Magikarp

5km Pokémon Eggs:

Any of the 2km Pokémon can hatch from a 5km Egg, plus:

Ekans, Sandshrew, Nidoran♀, Nidoran♂, Vulpix, Oddish, Paras, Venonat, Diglett, Meowth, Psyduck, Mankey, Growlithe, Poliwag, Abra, Machop, Bellsprout, Tentacool, Ponyta, Slowpoke, Magnemite, Farfetch'd, Doduo, Seel, Grimer, Shellder, Gastly, Drowzee, Krabby, Voltorb, Exeggcute, Cubone, Lickitung, Koffing, Rhyhorn, Tangela, Kangaskhan, Horsea, Goldeen, Staryu, Tauros, Porygon

10km Pokémon Eggs:

Any of the 2km or 5km Pokémon can hatch from a 10km Egg, plus:

Onix, Hitmonlee, Hitmonchan, Chansey, Mr. Mime, Scyther, Jynx, Electabuzz, Magmar, Pinsir, Lapras, Eevee, Omanyte, Kabuto, Aerodactyl, Snorlax, Dratini

Yes, it can be a letdown to get 2km Pokémon inside 5km & 10km Eggs. Just be prepared for it! The bright spot is that you still get a lot of XP, Candy, and Stardust!

Oh?

EXPERIENCE VALUES

Experience (or XP) is a unit of measure inside Pokémon GO that tracks your progression through the game. The XP Leveling system is very similar to the system used in the Pokémon role-playing video games. As you gain XP, you will eventually gain Levels. Gaining higher Levels opens more doors of opportunity for you inside game.

Here are some ways that XP can be gained inside the game.

Checking PokéStops

Normal PokéStop—50 XP, plus about 3 items

Large PokéStop—100 XP, plus about 6 items

Throwing Bonus

Curveball—10 XP

Nice Throw—10 XP

Great Throw—50 XP

Excellent Throw—100 XP

Catching and Evolving Pokémon

Pokémon Caught—100 XP

New Pokémon Caught—500 XP

Evolving Pokémon—500 XP

Evolving a New Pokémon—1,000 XP

Hatching Pokémon Eggs

2km Egg—200 XP

5km Egg—500 XP

10km Egg—1,000 XP

Gym Battles

Against Allies—Varies depending on Ally Level—10 XP to 50 XP

Battling at a Rival Gym—Varies depending on Level—10XP to 100 XP

Defeating a Trainer at a Gym—10XP to 150 XP *(This can increase based on the number of Pokémon defending the gym)*

Bonus for Defeating All Pokémon in a Gym—50 XP

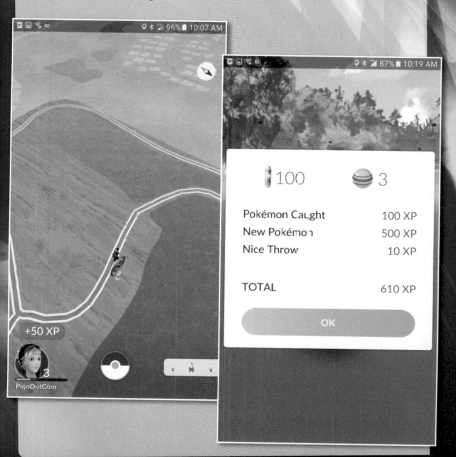

This book is not sponsored, endorsed by, or otherwise affiliated with any companies or the products featured in the book. This is not an official publication.

85

POKÉMON GO PLUS

The Pokémon GO Plus is an accessory that you will be able to purchase from retailers to enhance Pokémon GO. In June 2016, places like GameStop and Amazon were taking pre-orders for these accessories. Even though the availability date was unknown, the pre-orders sold out! And this was before Pokémon GO was even released.

So what is Pokémon GO Plus?

The GO Plus is a portable device that will enable Pokémon GO players to enjoy the game even while

they're not looking at their mobile devices. The GO Plus connects to a smartphone via Bluetooth and notifies the player about events in the game—such as the appearance of a Pokémon nearby—using LED and vibration. In addition, players can catch Pokémon or perform other simple actions by pressing the button on the device.

Nintendo claims you will be able to collect Pokéballs, Razz Berries, Pokémon Eggs, and other items at set PokéStop locations without having to look at your smart phone.

It appears the Pokémon GO Plus is worn as a bracelet, but also has a belt clip. The device will cost you about $35 when it eventually hits streets.

We're not sure how well this device will work, but we know they're going to sell like hotcakes when they hit retailers. People that have guaranteed pre-orders are currently listing these for about $150 on eBay, and they are selling! We will hopefully have a detailed review for you in an upcoming Pojo Pokémon book.

FACT OR FICTION?

With so much information out there about Pokémon GO, it can be hard to figure out what information is real and what isn't. So we sent out our own myth busters to get the facts for you.

You can actually begin with a Pikachu as your starting Pokémon.
Fact: By walking away from the first three Pokémon a total of three times, you can choose Pikachu the fourth time.

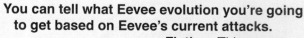

You can tell what Eevee evolution you're going to get based on Eevee's current attacks.
Fiction: This was an early rumor that turned out to be false. You can rename your Eevee though, and force the evolution you want.

If you want Ghost Pokémon, you should visit a graveyard.
Fiction: The people behind Pokémon GO have said they were very careful not to put Ghost Pokémon near graveyards or cemeteries because they don't want people going there for that purpose.

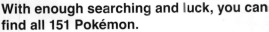

With enough searching and luck, you can find all 151 Pokémon.
Fiction: For the moment, at least. As of this writing, Articuno, Zapdos, Moltres, Ditto, Mewtwo, and Mew are all unavailable. We think they will be releasing them for certain events, but right now we don't have any information how they will be released.

More Pokémon spawn in crowded places.
Fact: Anywhere there are lots of people, there are likely to be lots of cell phone towers. The higher the cellular density is, the more likely Pokémon will spawn in that area.

If your friend found a rare Pokémon, you should go there too if you want to find it.
Fact: Most rare Pokémon do have particular places they will spawn. The only problem is you won't know how often or when they will spawn next. If your friend caught a Charizard over at the skate park, there is a good chance that a Charizard will spawn there again. But it could be hours or days before it happens again.

You can rename Pokémon something cool and everyone will see it at Gyms.
Fiction: When you rename a Pokémon, only you see the rename. People who see it in a Gym will only see the actual name of the Pokémon.

If you miss with a Pokéball, tap it quickly to get it back.
Fiction: Once you throw it, you're not getting it back, no matter how much you tap it.

You can catch different Pokémon in different weather. For example, Water Pokémon when it rains, or Electric Pokémon during a thunderstorm.
Fiction: There is no evidence that the weather around you affects what Pokémon you get. But your climate does effect the Pokémon you find. Grass and Bug Pokémon will be found near golf courses and parks. Fire and Rock Pokémon

are found in deserts. Water Pokémon are found near coastal land.

Some Pokémon are more likely to spawn during the day or at night.

Fact: Certain Pokémon, like Ghost and Fairy Pokémon, tend to spawn more at night. Your area will also likely have some Pokémon particular to your location that you see more during the day or night. That means if you want to "catch 'em all," you'll have to venture out at different times of the day.

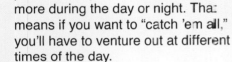

POKÉMON COMBAT CHART

"Rock-Paper-Scizors"

Battling in Pokémon is a lot like playing a giant version of "Rock-Paper-Scissors." But in Pokémon there are actually 18 Pokémon Types to contend with. Some matchups are simple to figure out: Water Pokémon are strong against Fire. Fire is strong versus Grass. Ground types are great against Electric types. But when it comes to types like Bug, Rock, Ghost, and Ice, you may be left scratching your head.

All Pokémon and their moves are assigned certain "Types." Each type has strengths and weaknesses in both attacks and defense. When attacking, you want to use attacks that give you an advantage over your opponent.

Example of Using This Chart: The Gym you are attacking has a Flareon, a Fire type. You attack with your Squirtle, a Water type. You look at the chart and it shows a "+"—that means your attack will be super effective, doing twice the normal damage. If you attack Flareon with Caterpie, a Bug type Pokémon, you see a "-"—so you will only do ½ damage. An "=" means your attack will not be very effective at all, doing almost no damage. Empty squares mean your attacks will do normal damage.

Some Pokémon, like Rhydon, are actually two types (Rhydon is both Ground and Rock). That can come in handy when attacking, but that also leaves him doubly exposed when defending Gyms.

Another thing to know is that your Pokémon can earn a "Same Type Attack Bonus," or STAB. As the name implies, this increases the power of the move if the attacking Pokémon has the same type as the move used (for example, a Fire-type Pokémon using a Fire-type move). The attack will be amplified by 50%.

Our Combat Chart does not have Fairy Types. Fairy types were added in Generation VI. We are not sure which Combat Chart Pokémon GO is using. Just in case: Fairy types are effective against Fighting and Dragon, and weak against Poison and Steel.

Defending Pokémon Type

Your Attack Type ↓ \ Defending →	Normal	Fire	Water	Electric	Grass	Ice	Fighting	Poison	Ground	Flying	Psychic	Bug	Rock	Ghost	Dragon	Dark	Steel
Normal													-	=			-
Fire		-	-		+	+						+	-		-		+
Water		+	-		-				+				+		-		
Electric			+	-	-				=	+					-		
Grass		-	+		-			-	+	-		-	+		-		-
Ice		-	-		+	-			+	+					+		-
Fighting	+					+		-		-	-	-	+	=		+	+
Poison					+			-	-				-	-			=
Ground		+		+	-			+		=		-	+				+
Flying				-	+		+					+	-				-
Psychic							+	+			-					=	-
Bug		-			+		-	-		-	+			-		+	-
Rock		+				+	-		-	+		+					-
Ghost	=										+			+		-	-
Dragon															+		-
Dark							-				+			+		-	-
Steel		-	-	-		+							+				-

Physical attacks are in red

Special attacks are in blue

Damage for **+** attacks are multiplied by 2

Attack Type/Pokémon Type match: multipled by 1.5

Damage for **-** attacks: multiplied by 0.5

Damage for **=** attacks: multiplied by 0

THE FUTURE OF POKÉMON GO?

Many things get teased at Comic-Con in San Diego every year: future movie releases, future TV show releases, future game releases, etc. In July of 2016, John Hanke, the CEO of Niantic (creators of Pokémon GO), took the stage on the last day of Comic-Con and teased some information about the future of Pokémon GO.

First, he revealed the leaders of each Pokémon GO Team:

- Team Mystic—Blanche

- Team Valor—Candela

- Team Instinct—Spark

Candela — Valor

Blanche — Mystic

Spark — Instinct

Hanke also acknowledged there are more "Easter Eggs" in the game beyond renaming your Eevee! Who's going to find them first?

The CEO then teased some other ideas they're considering in the near future:

- More Pokémon being added, beyond Generation I
- Adding Pokémon Centers
- Breeding Pokémon
- Trading Pokémon with friends
- Giving new/more capabilities to PokéStops
- And unleashing more Legendary Pokémon

Hanke made it clear that, first and foremost, they want to release the game worldwide, and then squash all the bugs that have plagued the game in the first few weeks after release. He added, "We expect Pokémon GO to run for years and we are going to continue to invest in it in that way."

So keep walking, and keep tossing those Pokéballs! There are plenty of Pokémon out there, and more coming!

THE POKÉDEX

Introduction

The Pokédex is a comprehensive Pokémon encyclopedia. The Pokédex contains a database of statistics on all Pokémon. These statistics include: Height, Weight, Type, Evolutions, Weaknesses, Hit Points, Attacks, Defense, Speed, Special Attacks, etc. Every single Pokémon has a reference number in the Pokédex, starting with Bulbasaur at #1. The Pokédex is used in both the Pokémon video games and in the Pokémon anime, and now it's being put to use in Pokémon GO.

In Pokémon GO, there are currently 151 Pokémon. These Pokémon are considered Generation I Pokémon, which were originally found in the very first Pokémon video games— Pokémon Red and Blue in 1998.

Inside Pokémon GO, the Pokédex shows you which Pokémon you have seen and which Pokémon you have

Pojo's Power Ratings are based on a 1 to 5 scale.

1 is Awful.

3 is Average.

5 is Amazing!

These rankings are based on Base Statistics. Almost all Pokémon can powered-up into forces to be reckoned with!

caught. If you haven't seen a specific numbered Pokémon, there will be no information about that Pokémon. Detailed information about each Pokémon is added to the Pokédex as you catch them.

Our detailed Pokédex can be helpful in Pokémon GO. It can be especially useful for understanding Pokémon Types and Pokémon Evolutions. Evolution lines will help you decide if you want to evolve certain Pokémon, while knowing the Pokémon Types will help you prepare for Gym Battles. Consult with the "Pokémon Combat Chart" in this book to help you understand effective Pokémon attacks before you head into Gym battles! Taking the right Pokémon with you will definitely be the difference between winning and losing.

Pojo Note: There are currently 729 Pokémon in the Pokémon Universe. Over the last 20 years, Pokémon has evolved into VI generations of Pokémon. We expect The Pokémon Company to slowly add in more Pokémon, Generation by Generation. Maybe we will see Generation II sometime in 2017?

#1 Bulbasaur

Type: Grass

Evolves from: n/a

Pojo's Rating: 2

#2 Ivysaur

Type: Grass

Evolves from: Bulbasaur

Pojo's Rating: 3

#3 Venusaur

Type: Grass

Evolves from: Ivysaur

Pojo's Rating: 5

#4 Charmander

Type: Fire

Evolves from: n/a

Pojo's Rating: 2

#5 Charmeleon

Type: Fire

Evolves from: Charmander

Pojo's Rating: 3

#6 Charizard

Type: Fire

Evolves from: Charmeleon

Pojo's Rating: 5

#7 Squirtle

Type: Water

Evolves from: n/a

Pojo's Rating: 2

#8 Wartortle

Type: Water

Evolves from: Squirtle

Pojo's Rating: 3

#9 Blastoise

Type: Water

Evolves from: Wartortle

Pojo's Rating: 5

#10 Caterpie

Type: Bug

Evolves from: n/a

Pojo's Rating: 1

#11 Metapod

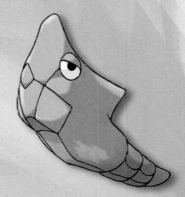

Type: Bug

Evolves from: Caterpie

Pojo's Rating: 1

#12 Butterfree

Type: Bug

Evolves from: Metapod

Pojo's Rating: 3

#13 Weedle

Type: Bug/Poison

Evolves from: n/a

Pojo's Rating: 1

#14 Kakuna

Type: Bug/Poison

Evolves from: Weedle

Pojo's Rating: 1

#15 Beedrill

Type: Bug/Poison

Evolves from: Kakuna

Pojo's Rating: 3

#16 PIDGEY

Type: Normal/Flying

Evolves from: n/a

Pojo's Rating: 1

#17 PIDGEOTTO

Type: Normal/Flying

Evolves from: Pidgey

Pojo's Rating: 2

#18 PIDGEOT

Type: Normal/Flying

Evolves from: Pidgeotto

Pojo's Rating: 3

#19 Rаттата

Type: Normal

Evolves from: n/a

Pojo's Rating: 1

#20 Rатıсате

Type: Normal

Evolves from: Rattata

Pojo's Rating: 3

#21 Spearow

Type: Normal/Flying

Evolves from: n/a

Pojo's Rating: 1

#22 Fearow

Type: Normal/Flying

Evolves from: Spearow

Pojo's Rating: 3

#23 Ekans

Type: Poison

Evolves from: n/a

Pojo's Rating: 1

#24 Arbok

Type: Poison

Evolves from: Ekans

Pojo's Rating: 3

#25 Pikachu

Type: Electric

Evolves from: n/a

Pojo's Rating: 2

#26 Raichu

Type: Electric

Evolves from: Pikachu

Pojo's Rating: 3

#27 Sandshrew

Type: Ground

Evolves from: n/a

Pojo's Rating: 2

#28 Sandslash

Type: Ground

Evolves from: Sandshrew

Pojo's Rating: 3

#29 Nidoran ♀

Type: Poison

Evolves from: n/a

Pojo's Rating: 1

#30 Nidorina

Type: Poison

Evolves from: Nidoran ♀

Pojo's Rating: 3

#31 Nidoqueen

Type: Poison/Ground

Evolves from: Nidorina

Pojo's Rating: 4

#32 Nidoran♂

Type: Poison

Evolves from: n/a

Pojo's Rating: 1

#33 Nidorino

Type: Poison

Evolves from: Nidoran♂

Pojo's Rating: 3

#34 Nidoking

Type: Poison/Ground

Evolves from: Nidorino

Pojo's Rating: 4

#35 Clefairy

Type: Fairy

Evolves from: n/a

Pojo's Rating: 2

#36 Clefable

Type: Fairy

Evolves from: Clefairy

Pojo's Rating: 4

#37 Vulpix

Type: Fire

Evolves from: n/a

Pojo's Rating: 2

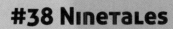

#38 Ninetales

Type: Fire

Evolves from: Vulpix

Pojo's Rating: 4

#39 Jigglypuff

Type: Normal/Fairy

Evolves from: n/a

Pojo's Rating: 1

#40 Wigglytuff

Type: Normal/Fairy

Evolves from: Jigglypuff

Pojo's Rating: 3

#41 Zubat

Type: Poison/Flying

Evolves from: n/a

Pojo's Rating: 1

#42 Golbat

Type: Poison/Flying

Evolves from: Zubat

Pojo's Rating: 3

#43 ODDISH

Type: Grass/Poison

Evolves from: n/a

Pojo's Rating: 2

#44 GLOOM

Type: Grass/Poison

Evolves from: Oddish

Pojo's Rating: 3

#45 VILEPLUME

Type: Grass/Poison

Evolves from: Gloom

Pojo's Rating: 3

#46 Paras

Type: Bug/Grass

Evolves from: n/a

Pojo's Rating: 2

#47 Parasect

Type: Bug/Grass

Evolves from: Paras

Pojo's Rating: 3

#48 Venonat

Type: Bug/Poison

Evolves from: n/a

Pojo's Rating: 2

#49 Venomoth

Type: Bug/Poison

Evolves from: Venonat

Pojo's Rating: 3

#50 Diglett

Type: Ground

Evolves from: n/a

Pojo's Rating: 1

#51 Dugtrio

Type: Ground

Evolves from: Diglett

Pojo's Rating: 3

#52 Meowth

Type: Normal

Evolves from: n/a

Pojo's Rating: 2

#53 Persian

Type: Normal

Evolves from: Meowth

Pojo's Rating: 3

#54 Psyduck

Type: Water

Evolves from: n/a

Pojo's Rating: 2

#55 Golduck

Type: Water

Evolves from: Psyduck

Pojo's Rating: 4

#56 Mankey

Type: Fighting

Evolves from: n/a

Pojo's Rating: 2

#57 Primeape

Type: Fighting

Evolves from: Mankey

Pojo's Rating: 3

#58 Growlithe

Type: Fire

Evolves from: n/a

Pojo's Rating: 2

#59 Arcanine

Type: Fire

Evolves from: Growlithe

Pojo's Rating: 5

#60 Poliwag

Type: Water

Evolves from: n/a

Pojo's Rating: 2

#61 Poliwhirl

Type: Water

Evolves from: Poliwag

Pojo's Rating: 3

#62 Poliwrath

Type: Water/Fighting

Evolves from: Poliwhirl

Pojo's Rating: 4

#63 Aʙʀᴀ

Type: Psychic

Evolves from: n/a

Pojo's Rating: 2

#64 Kᴀᴅᴀʙʀᴀ

Type: Psychic

Evolves from: Abra

Pojo's Rating: 3

#65 Aʟᴀᴋᴀᴢᴀᴍ

Type: Psychic

Evolves from: Kadabra

Pojo's Rating: 4

#66 Machop

Type: Fighting

Evolves from: n/a

Pojo's Rating: 2

#67 Machoke

Type: Fighting

Evolves from: Machop

Pojo's Rating: 3

#68 Machamp

Type: Fighting

Evolves from: Machoke

Pojo's Rating: 4

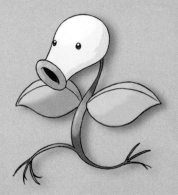

#69 Bellsprout

Type: Grass/Poison

Evolves from: n/a

Pojo's Rating: 2

#70 Weepinbell

Type: Grass/Poison

Evolves from: Bellsprout

Pojo's Rating: 3

#71 Victreebel

Type: Grass/Poison

Evolves from: Bellsprout

Pojo's Rating: 3

#72 Tentacool

Type: Water/Poison

Evolves from: n/a

Pojo's Rating: 2

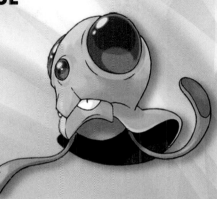

#73 Tentacruel

Type: Water/Poison

Evolves from: Tentacool

Pojo's Rating: 4

#74 Geodude

Type: Rock/Ground

Evolves from: n/a

Pojo's Rating: 2

#75 Graveler

Type: Rock/Ground

Evolves from: Geodude

Pojo's Rating: 3

#76 Golem

Type: Rock/Ground

Evolves from: Graveler

Pojo's Rating: 3

#77 Ponyta

Type: Fire

Evolves from: n/a

Pojo's Rating: 3

#78 Rapidash

Type: Fire

Evolves from: Ponyta

Pojo's Rating: 4

#79 Slowpoke

Type: Water/Psychic

Evolves from: n/a

Pojo's Rating: 2

#80 Slowbro

Type: Water/Psychic

Evolves from: Slowpoke

Pojo's Rating: 4

#81 Magnemite

Type: Electric/Steel

Evolves from: n/a

Pojo's Rating: 2

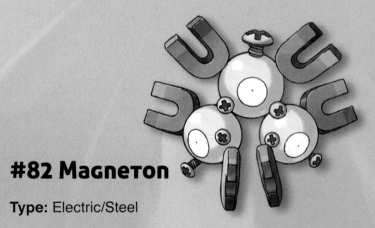

#82 Magneton

Type: Electric/Steel

Evolves from: Magnemite

Pojo's Rating: 3

#83 Farfetch'd

Type: Normal/Flying

Evolves from: n/a

Pojo's Rating: 2

#84 Doduo

Type: Normal/Flying

Evolves from: n/a

Pojo's Rating: 2

#85 Dodrio

Type: Normal/Flying

Evolves from: Doduo

Pojo's Rating: 3

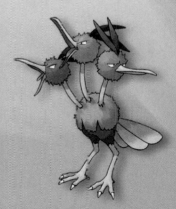

#86 Seel

Type: Water

Evolves from: n/a

Pojo's Rating: 2

#87 Dewgong

Type: Water

Evolves from: Seel

Pojo's Rating: 4

#88 Grimer

Type: Poison

Evolves from: n/a

Pojo's Rating: 2

#89 Muk

Type: Muk

Evolves from: Grimer

Pojo's Rating: 4

#90 Shellder

Type: Water

Evolves from: n/a

Pojo's Rating: 2

#91 Cloyster

Type: Water/Ice

Evolves from: Shellder

Pojo's Rating: 4

#92 GASTLY

Type: Ghost/Poison

Evolves from: n/a

Pojo's Rating: 2

#93 HAUNTER

Type: Ghost/Poison

Evolves from: Gastly

Pojo's Rating: 3

#94 GENGAR

Type: Ghost/Poison

Evolves from: Haunter

Pojo's Rating: 5

#95 Onix

Type: Rock/Ground

Evolves from: n/a

Pojo's Rating: 2

#96 Drowzee

Type: Psychic

Evolves from: n/a

Pojo's Rating: 2

#97 Hypno

Type: Psychic

Evolves from: Drowzee

Pojo's Rating: 3

#98 Krabby

Type: Water

Evolves from: n/a

Pojo's Rating: 2

#99 Kingler

Type: Water

Evolves from: Krabby

Pojo's Rating: 3

#100 Voltorb

Type: Electric

Evolves from: n/a

Pojo's Rating: 2

#101 Electrode

Type: Electric

Evolves from: Voltorb

Pojo's Rating: 3

#102 Exeggcute

Type: Grass/Psychic

Evolves from: n/a

Pojo's Rating: 2

#103 Exeggutor

Type: Grass/Psychic

Evolves from: Exeggcute

Pojo's Rating: 4

#104 Cubone

Type: Ground

Evolves from: n/a

Pojo's Rating: 3

#105 Marowak

Type: Ground

Evolves from: Cubone

Pojo's Rating: 3

#106
Hitmonlee

Type: Fighting

Evolves from: n/a

Pojo's Rating: 3

#107
Hitmonchan

Type: Fighting

Evolves from: n/a

Pojo's Rating: 3

#108 Lickitung

Type: Normal

Evolves from: n/a

Pojo's Rating: 2

#109 Koffing

Type: Poison

Evolves from: n/a

Pojo's Rating: 2

#110 Weezing

Type: Poison

Evolves from: Koffing

Pojo's Rating: 4

#111 Rhyhorn

Type: Ground/Rock

Evolves from: n/a

Pojo's Rating: 3

#112 Rhydon

Type: Ground/Rock

Evolves from: Rhyhorn

Pojo's Rating: 4

#113 Chansey

Type: Normal

Evolves from: n/a

Pojo's Rating: 3

#114 Tangela

Type: Grass

Evolves from: n/a

Pojo's Rating: 3

#115 Kangaskhan

Type: Normal

Evolves from: n/a

Pojo's Rating: 4

#116 Horsea

Type: Water

Evolves from: n/a

Pojo's Rating: 2

#117 Seadra

Type: Water

Evolves from: Horsea

Pojo's Rating: 3

#118 Goldeen

Type: Water

Evolves from: n/a

Pojo's Rating: 2

#119 Seaking

Type: Water

Evolves from: Goldeen

Pojo's Rating: 4

#120 Staryu

Type: Water

Evolves from: n/a

Pojo's Rating: 2

#121 Starmie

Type: Water/Psychic

Evolves from: Staryu

Pojo's Rating: 4

#122 Mr. Mime

Type: Psychic/Fairy

Evolves from: n/a

Pojo's Rating: 3

#123 Scyther

Type: Bug/Flying

Evolves from: n/a

Pojo's Rating: 4

#124 Jynx

Type: Ice/Psychic

Evolves from: n/a

Pojo's Rating: 3

#125 Electabuzz

Type: Electric

Evolves from: n/a

Pojo's Rating: 4

#126 Magmar

Type: Fire

Evolves from: n/a

Pojo's Rating: 4

#127 Pinsir

Type: Bug

Evolves from: n/a

Pojo's Rating: 4

#128 Tauros

Type: Normal

Evolves from: n/a

Pojo's Rating: 4

#129 Magikarp

Type: Water

Evolves from: n/a

Pojo's Rating: 1

#130 Gyarados

Type: Water/Flying

Evolves from: Magikarp

Pojo's Rating: 5

#131 Lapras

Type: Water/Ice

Evolves from: n/a

Pojo's Rating: 5

#132 DITTO

Type: Normal

Evolves from: n/a

Pojo's Rating: 2

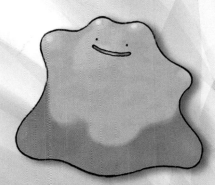

#133 Eevee

Type: Normal

Evolves from: n/a

Pojo's Rating: 2

#134 Vaporeon

Type: Water

Evolves from: Eevee

Pojo's Rating: 4

#135 Jolteon

Type: Electric

Evolves from: Eevee

Pojo's Rating: 4

#136 Flareon

Type: Fire

Evolves from: Eevee

Pojo's Rating: 4

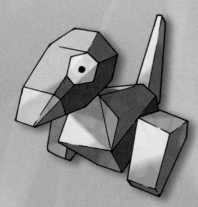

#137 Porygon

Type: Normal

Evolves from: n/a

Pojo's Rating: 3

#138 Omanyte

Type: Rock/Water

Evolves from: n/a

Pojo's Rating: 3

#139 Omastar

Type: Rock/Water

Evolves from: Omanyte

Pojo's Rating: 4

#140 Kabuto

Type: Rock/Water

Evolves from: n/a

Pojo's Rating: 2

#141 Kabutops

Type: Rock/Water

Evolves from: Kabuto

Pojo's Rating: 4

#142 Aerodactyl

Type: Rock/Flying

Evolves from: n/a

Pojo's Rating: 4

#143 Snorlax

Type: Normal

Evolves from: n/a

Pojo's Rating: 5

#144 ARTICUNO

Type: Ice/Flying

Evolves from: n/a

Pojo's Rating: 5

#145 ZAPDOS

Type: Electric/Flying

Evolves from: n/a

Pojo's Rating: 5

#146 MOLTRES

Type: Fire/Flying

Evolves from: n/a

Pojo's Rating: 5

#147 Dratini

Type: Dragon

Evolves from: n/a

Pojo's Rating: 2

#148 Dragonair

Type: Dragon

Evolves from: Dratini

Pojo's Rating: 3

#149 Dragonite

Type: Dragon/Flying

Evolves from: Dragonair

Pojo's Rating: 5

#150 Mewtwo

Type: Psychic

Evolves from: n/a

Pojo's Rating: 5

#151 Mew

Type: Psychic

Evolves from: n/a

Pojo's Rating: 5